UNLOCK THE POWER OF NOW

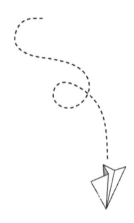

Discover the Secrets to Let Go of the Past, Stop Worrying About the Future, and Finding Joy in Every Moment

Rafael Lumnis

TABLE OF CONTENTS

INTRODUCTION

The future doesn't exist. Need proof? Let me show you. I'm about to give you a few words that, as of now, are still in the future. Pay close attention to them. Here they are: THESE ARE THE WORDS. The moment you read them, they became the present—something happening here and now. And just as quickly, they've slipped into the past, now merely a memory of something you just read. Do you see how it works? What we call "the future" exists only as an idea in our minds. Tomorrow is just a word, while today is the only reality we can truly experience.

Even if plans for the future seem as certain as the sunrise, the truth is we have no control over them. Our lives are made up of a series of "nows," not "somedays." The future is elusive, and the only reality you can claim is the one happening at this very moment.

Do you know what else is just as intangible? The past. For many of us, the past is a burden we carry on our backs. Yet, do we realize that we lack the power to change anything that's already happened? Every decision, every mistake, and even every joyful moment from the past is gone—irreversible and unchangeable. Dwelling on those painful moments and errors traps us, preventing us from moving forward. The past is beyond our control, and reliving it accomplishes nothing but wasting time. True freedom comes when you let go of the past. What truly matters is what you do right now, and in that lies your real power.

That's why success, fulfillment, and genuine joy aren't found in chasing wealth, power, or titles. Those pursuits are illusions, always just out of reach. What truly matters is the ability to live in the present. Real happiness isn't about what you own but about how you experience each moment. It's how you wake up and commit to being present, engaged, and alive. You don't need to wait for "the perfect moment" because that moment is already here. The choice is yours, and your life is the sum of the decisions you make every day.

When you free yourself from the past and stop worrying about what might happen, you'll discover that what truly matters is the quality of the moments you experience here and now.

"

As long as we live, there's no point in worrying
about the future because we have no control over
it. Each day is a new beginning"

~ Eckhart Tolle

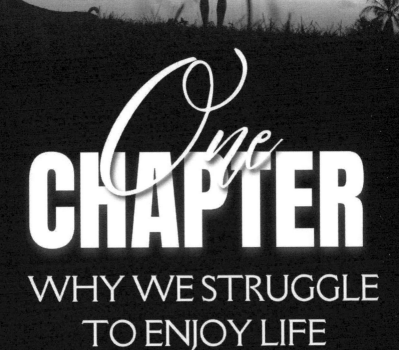

CHAPTER *One*

WHY WE STRUGGLE TO ENJOY LIFE

- How the Past Shapes Our Lives
- The Future That Frightens Us
- What Does It Mean to Live in the Now?

How the Past Shapes Our Lives

Our mistakes and failures often become a heavy burden, like a backpack filled with stones that we carry everywhere we go. Every misstep, every decision we regret, seems to weigh down our daily lives. Instead of treating these experiences as lessons that can enrich us, we allow them to define our worth. For many people, mistakes become a wall that blocks any further progress.

Take Thomas Edison's story as a prime example. When he invented the light bulb, he faced thousands of failures before achieving success. Each failure could have discouraged him or convinced him that he wasn't good enough. Yet, he famously said, *"I have not failed. I've just found 10,000 ways that won't work."* Edison understood that mistakes are a natural part of the process, not its end. Had he let his past failures define his future, he would never have changed the world. But too often, we do the opposite—we stay trapped by our failures. Instead of moving forward, we keep looking back, clinging to moments that no longer hold any power.

Memories from the past, especially painful ones, can become a trap that freezes our ability to find joy in the present. When we repeatedly revisit moments of loss, disappointment, or struggle, our thoughts spiral into the past, robbing us of the chance to embrace what's happening now. It's like looking through old photographs that stir up longing for something that's gone, blinding us to the beauty of what we currently have. Life isn't meant to be a collection of old pictures but a series of fresh, vibrant experiences. When we live in memories, we forget that the present offers us the opportunity to create new stories. Instead of dwelling on the past, we should treat life as a blank canvas, ready to be painted anew every day.

Unresolved issues from the past—unspoken words, lingering conflicts, or abandoned dreams—can deeply affect our psyche. They're like a forgotten task on your desk, constantly demanding your attention. These unresolved matters feed into our subconscious, influencing our thoughts and decisions. Rather than living fully, we orbit around these unfinished pieces of our past. Think of Hamlet, Shakespeare's tragic character, who spent much of his life consumed by the duty of revenge. His inability to move on from his unresolved obligations ultimately led to his downfall. Similarly, we, like Hamlet, often remain tethered to unresolved issues that hold us back instead of setting us free.

Unlock the Power of Now

The past can become a mental trap when we let it control our thoughts and emotions. But liberation is possible. The key lies in recognizing that the past only holds power over us if we allow it to. Releasing ourselves from its grip requires forgiving ourselves and others, letting go of guilt, and embracing the idea that each moment is a fresh start. Perhaps the most crucial step is accepting that life doesn't move backward and that every new moment is an opportunity for renewal. As Eckhart Tolle wisely said, *"The past is just a story we keep telling ourselves. The future is something we create, starting now."*

By consciously choosing what to carry forward from our past and what to leave behind, we reclaim true freedom.

"

"I have not failed. I've just found 10,000 ways that won't work" ~ **Thomas Edison**

The Future That Frightens Us

The fear of the unknown is one of the most powerful forces that keeps us trapped in a cage of uncertainty. We live in a world where the future feels like an unexplored black hole, and we, like characters in a horror movie, are afraid to look into its depths. It's natural for the unknown to cause hesitation, but we cannot let this fear control our lives. The future is elusive—not because it's inherently bad, but simply because it's unpredictable. We have no control over it, and the more we try to grasp it, the more it slips away. Instead of being paralyzed by fear, we should learn to view the future as something to shape, not something to dread.

Take Jeff Bezos as an example. He started Amazon with a simple idea in a garage. When he thought about the future, he wasn't immobilized by fear. His vision, though ambitious, was grounded in the present. Rather than obsessing over how far he could go, he focused on daily progress. Bezos understood that the future isn't something to control but something to build, step by step. His ability to overcome the fear of the unknown allowed him to take risks, ultimately creating one of the most powerful companies in the world. Perhaps it was not the absence of fear but his willingness to face it that fueled his success.

Self-fulfillment is often overshadowed by the pursuit of long-term goals, making it easy to overlook the joy of what we have right now. In our race toward an ideal future, we forget that happiness isn't about postponing life for later. While long-term goals are valuable foundations, they shouldn't eclipse the daily joys already within reach. Here lies the paradox: when we fixate too much on what's ahead, we lose sight of the happiness that exists in the present. For instance, if we spend our entire lives waiting for the "perfect moment" to start a career, we delay joy indefinitely—and when that moment finally arrives, we might realize we've forgotten how to enjoy it.

Trying to overcontrol the future is like obsessively chasing your own shadow. We attempt to predict every scenario, calculate risks, and plan every detail, only to find that the future rarely unfolds as we imagined. Instead of controlling, we should learn to act in harmony with what is here and now. The key is accepting that not everything can be predicted or controlled. Reality is fluid, and our plans are often subject to unpredictable circumstances. This unpredictability, far from being a weakness, might be what makes life interesting—it allows us to adapt, create, and grow. A life without risk or uncharted paths would be like a game without excitement.

Unlock the Power of Now

Remember, fear of the future doesn't have to paralyze us. Instead, we can embrace it as a companion that highlights new challenges. Fear isn't an enemy; it's a tool—a signal that something exciting might be ahead. When we stop trying to control everything and open ourselves to what life brings, we may find that unpredictability is our greatest strength. As Steve Jobs once said, *"Your time is limited, so don't waste it living someone else's life."* Focus on the present, and the future will naturally become the next chapter in your unique story.

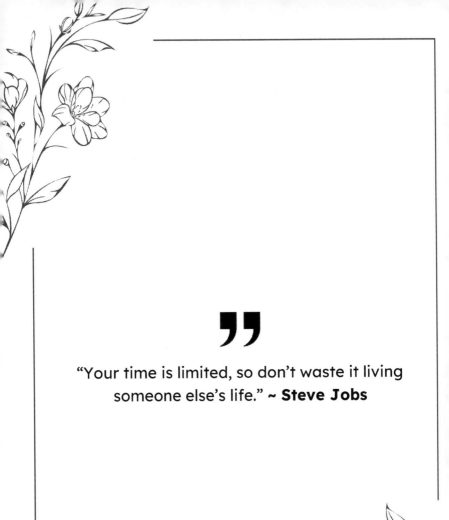

"Your time is limited, so don't waste it living someone else's life." ~ **Steve Jobs**

What Does It Mean to Live in the Now?

To be present in each moment means to pause and fully experience what is happening now, without being distracted by thoughts of the past or future. It's not just about physical presence; it's about engaging your mind and heart fully in whatever you're doing. Living in the now is about consciously experiencing every moment without judgment or comparison. It's the art of immersing yourself in the present—whether it's something as simple as enjoying a cup of coffee or as meaningful as having a heartfelt conversation with someone close. It's recognizing that every moment holds value, and fully embracing it is the key to inner peace and joy.

Incorporating mindfulness into daily life may seem challenging in a world full of distractions. However, mindfulness is nothing more than being aware of what's happening right now—in your thoughts, emotions, and body. It's the ability to notice details you'd typically overlook: the rustling of the wind, the scent of rain, or the warmth of sunlight on your skin. Practicing mindfulness means fully living in the moment, without judgment or overanalyzing. This can be achieved in many ways, from simple breathing exercises and meditation to everyday activities. For instance, during a walk, instead of thinking about your to-do list, you can focus on your steps, the surrounding sounds, scents, and every detail of the moment.

Relaxation techniques and breathing play a significant role in staying present. When our minds are overwhelmed by thoughts of the past or future, we can easily lose touch with the present. Breathing is one of the most powerful tools we have to reconnect with the here and now. A simple technique—conscious deep breathing, inhaling through the nose, holding for a moment, and slowly exhaling—can help relax the body and mind, releasing unnecessary stress. Breathing allows us to return to the present moment, giving us space to reflect, pause the rush of life, and feel a sense of control over what's happening within us.

Living in the now also means noticing the small pleasures life offers daily. Often, we rush through life without seeing the little moments that could bring us joy. A warm cup of tea on a cold morning, the laughter of a child, or the scent of your favorite flower—these small pleasures hold the power to create happiness when we start paying attention to them. We often forget that it's these small moments that make up our everyday joy. If we are mindful, we can realize that happiness doesn't always come from big events or achievements but from the simple, little things that fill our lives. It could be the smile on a loved one's face, the sound of rain on the roof, or the calm after a long day at work. When we begin to notice these fleeting but beautiful moments, our lives start to transform.

To be present in each moment, then, is the art of immersing yourself in the simplicity of life, requiring just one thing: a conscious choice. A conscious choice to be here and now, to breathe, to notice, and to appreciate what we already have. This is the key to inner peace, joy, and fulfillment—living in the now.

Two CHAPTER

BREAKING MENTAL HABITS

- Mental Traps That Hold Us Back
- Changing the Inner Dialogue
- Taking Control of Emotions

Mental Traps That Hold Us Back

The modern world, full of social media and constant access to information, feeds us comparisons. We are always faced with an image of a "better" version of ourselves—perfect, successful, with an ideal body and life. This constant comparison is a trap that limits our ability to be happy. You know the feeling—you scroll through Instagram, and everyone looks like they're from a fashion magazine, traveling to exotic places, living life to the fullest. And then the question arises: "Why don't I have all of that?" But the truth is, no one shows the full picture. Everyone is on a journey, there are no perfect people, and comparing ourselves to others leads to nothing but discomfort and dissatisfaction. How do we reduce this pressure? Simply stop comparing yourself to anyone else. Focus on your own progress, at your own pace. Remember, your goal is to become a better version of yourself, not a copy of someone else.

Perfectionism is another mental trap that can destroy our joy. Striving for perfection may seem ambitious at first glance, but in reality, it is a blockage. When we think everything must be perfect—our work, our life, our relationships—we become slaves to unrealistic expectations. And what happens when those expectations are not met? Feelings of failure, disappointment, and frustration. Perfectionism prevents us from enjoying what we've accomplished because we'll always see something that could be improved. If you're always looking for perfection, you'll miss the small successes that are the true source of happiness. The key is to accept that not everything must be perfect, and what we do has value regardless of how much it deviates from the "ideal image." In reality, it's our mistakes and imperfections that make us authentic.

Acceptance of our flaws and mistakes is one of the most important skills we can develop. Each of us makes mistakes—it's part of the human experience. Problems arise when we cannot accept these mistakes. Instead of treating them as lessons, we view them as shameful, something to be embarrassed about. But it is often our failures that lead us to the greatest discoveries. When we learn to accept our flaws, we begin to understand that they shape our uniqueness. Acceptance does not mean passivity, but the ability to learn and grow. Instead of complaining about our imperfections, consider what they might teach us. Many great figures, from Thomas Edison to Steve Jobs, spoke about how important it is to accept failure as an integral part of the path to success. Sometimes the greatest successes come from the biggest failures.

Unlock the Power of Now

Black-and-white thinking—everything or nothing—is another trap that limits our ability to grow and experience joy. This mindset leads to rigidity, inflexibility, and an unwillingness to change. If you think something is either perfect or a total failure, you probably will never feel satisfaction from the small progress you've made. The truth is, life is not just a series of black-and-white choices. Most things in life are shades of gray. Small steps forward are just as important as big successes. Instead of seeking perfection in every aspect of life, accept that small imperfections are part of the journey that leads to growth and satisfaction. Sometimes "good enough" is exactly what you need to feel fulfilled.

In conclusion, mental traps such as comparing ourselves to others, perfectionism, rejecting our mistakes, and black-and-white thinking can prevent us from enjoying life. Breaking free from these traps starts with acceptance—accepting ourselves, our imperfections, and the fact that life doesn't always need to be perfect to be valuable. It's a shift in perspective that allows for true freedom and joy in what we already have.

> "I could not change the past, but I could control my thoughts about the future."

~ Nelson Mandela

Changing the Inner Dialogue

It all starts with thoughts. What we think has a powerful impact on our emotions, which in turn shape our actions and decisions. Our thoughts can lift us up or bring us down. Here's an example: Imagine waking up with the belief that you have a tough day ahead, full of challenges beyond your control. You immediately start to feel stressed and anxious. But if, instead, you wake up thinking that you have control over your reaction to whatever the day brings, your emotions will instantly shift to a more positive state. Thoughts are like seeds; if we plant negative ones, negative emotions grow. If we plant thoughts full of optimism, joy and calm will bloom in our lives. Changing our inner dialogue is nothing more than a conscious decision to alter the way we think, thereby improving how we feel.

Techniques for shifting to more positive thinking are simple but require consistency. One of the most effective methods is "reframing." When thoughts of failure arise, replace them with more supportive and constructive ones. Instead of thinking, "I can't do this," try telling yourself, "This is a challenge, but I can handle it." Rather than focusing on past mistakes, start noticing what you can do now to improve the situation. Equally important is pausing when negative thoughts appear. Be aware of your inner dialogue—notice it and replace it with something more positive. It may sound trivial, but regular practice of such techniques has a huge impact on our daily well-being and approach to challenges.

Positive affirmations are one of the most powerful methods for changing the inner dialogue. We often don't realize how powerful the words we say to ourselves are. What we say has a profound effect on how we feel. Affirmations are short, positive statements that we repeat to strengthen our belief in ourselves and our capabilities. "I am strong enough to overcome any obstacle" or "Every day is a new opportunity for success"—these simple words can work wonders when we repeat them regularly. Affirmations may initially seem artificial, but over time, they begin to shape our reality, influencing our thinking and actions. It's helpful to start the day with a few positive affirmations that will lay the foundation for the entire day. These small rituals help build a strong sense of self-worth, which supports us through tough moments.

Building inner support is a key element in changing the inner dialogue. Creating daily affirmation rituals allows us to consistently strengthen our mental resilience. We can start with simple daily routines that help incorporate affirmations into our lives. For example, each time we look in the mirror and say, "I am ready for the challenges of today" or "I am good enough to achieve my goals," this can become a strong foundation for the start of the day. Over time, these words will become our inner truth, making us less susceptible to negative thoughts. Remember, changing the way we think takes time. It's a process that begins with small steps, but with each day, you'll become stronger and more resilient to doubts that may have previously held you back.

What can further support us in this process are inspirations from external sources—books, songs, or stories of other people. For instance, Nelson Mandela, who spent 27 years in prison, often emphasized how crucial maintaining a positive mindset was for him. In his autobiography *Long Walk to Freedom*, he wrote: "I could not change the past, but I could control my thoughts about the future." This mindset not only helped him survive the toughest times but also became the foundation of his later success. His story shows how vital it is to take control of what we think and how our mentality can influence our reality.

Changing our inner dialogue is a process that requires conscious effort and patience. Starting with affirmations, moving through daily rituals, and systematically reframing negative thoughts, we can gradually change the way we perceive ourselves and the world around us. Our thoughts have incredible power—they shape our emotions, and those, in turn, influence our actions. If we learn to control our thoughts, we will begin to live more fully, more consciously, and with a greater sense of fulfillment.

"

"Gratitude can turn an ordinary day into an extraordinary one, turn routine tasks into joy, and give meaning to moments."

~ Arthur Ward

Taking Control of Emotions

Emotions are like waves—they come and go, and their intensity varies. But how we respond to them shapes our perception of reality. For some, an emotional storm is an opportunity for reflection; for others, it becomes a reason to feel stuck. The key step in healing emotions is acceptance. It's not about pretending they don't exist or suppressing them, but about allowing them to be. As Brené Brown, an expert in human emotions, said: "You can't choose which emotions you want to numb and which to fully experience. If you numb sadness, you numb joy as well" (*The Gifts of Imperfection*). Acceptance is the first step in regaining balance because it allows us to see emotions for what they are—temporary states that do not define our identity.

Working on emotions is a process that requires active involvement, especially when it comes to negative emotions. One of the most effective ways to release negative emotions is by expressing them. Keeping a journal can be incredibly helpful in this. Writing gives our emotions space to exist. For example, we can ask ourselves, "Why am I feeling angry?", "What's causing my sadness?" or "Are my fears justified?". Writing allows us to name these feelings, and naming them is the first step in taming them. What's named becomes less terrifying. It's important to remember that expressing emotions doesn't have to be limited to writing. It can also be a conversation with a trusted person, creative self-expression through art, or even a simple walk that allows us to "digest" what's going on inside us.

However, releasing emotions is only part of the process. To truly change our mindset, it's helpful to cultivate a culture of gratitude. Gratitude acts like a lens that helps us focus on the good aspects of our lives, even in difficult times. Research conducted by the University of California, Davis, showed that people who practice daily gratitude experience greater life satisfaction and lower stress levels. All it takes is writing down three things you're grateful for each day—from small things, like a cup of hot coffee in the morning, to larger things, like support from friends. This simple ritual gradually changes how we view the world. As William Arthur Ward said: "Gratitude can turn an ordinary day into an extraordinary one, turn routine tasks into joy, and give meaning to moments."

Taking control of our emotions doesn't mean that we will suddenly stop feeling anger, sadness, or fear. It's about learning to manage them in a way that doesn't destroy us but supports us. Emotions are our teachers—they point to where we need change or attention. By accepting them, releasing them healthily, and learning gratitude, we begin to build the foundation for inner balance. Emotional balance is the key to a life of peace and fulfillment.

Three CHAPTER

PRACTICING THE PRESENT

- Daily Mindfulness Techniques
- Acceptance of Reality
- Creating Harmony with Life

"

"You can't stop the waves, but you can learn to surf." ~ **Jon Kabat-Zinn**

Daily Mindfulness Techniques

Mindfulness is the art of being present—experiencing the moment here and now, without judgment or analysis. In a world where multitasking is the norm, practicing mindfulness may seem like a luxury, but in reality, it's one of the simplest tools we have at our disposal. Introducing short mindfulness techniques into your daily life doesn't require special equipment or hours of silent meditation. All it takes is willingness and a few minutes each day.

Mindfulness meditation is a great way to bring mindfulness into your day. Start with simple 3-minute sessions. Sit comfortably, close your eyes, and focus on your breath. You don't need to control it—just observe how the air flows in and out of your lungs. If your thoughts start to wander (and they certainly will), gently redirect your attention back to your breath. This isn't a failure—this is the essence of mindfulness. As Jon Kabat-Zinn, the pioneer of mindfulness, said: "You can't stop the waves, but you can learn to surf." These short practices can be woven into any moment of the day—before an important meeting, during a lunch break, or even while waiting in line.

Another technique is breathing, which is often underestimated yet one of the most powerful tools we have. It's the bridge between body and mind. In moments of stress, try the 4-7-8 technique: inhale for 4 seconds, hold your breath for 7 seconds, and then exhale slowly for 8 seconds. This simple rhythm helps calm the nervous system, reduce tension, and improve focus. Regular breathing exercises not only help in times of crisis but also increase overall body and emotional awareness. As ancient yoga wisdom says: "When you control your breath, you control your mind."

Not everyone finds peace in meditation—and that's okay. Movement, such as walking, yoga, or dancing, can also become a form of meditation. The key is to focus on experiencing each moment of movement. During a walk, pay attention to the sensations in your feet as they touch the ground, the sound of the wind, or the noise around you. When practicing yoga, focus on how your body moves and the signals it sends. Movement brings us into a state where we let go of the need to control everything. We can simply be—without planning, analyzing, or striving—just experiencing.

Practicing mindfulness doesn't mean you'll always be able to live fully in the present. It's about returning to the here and now whenever you notice you've drifted into the past or future. Daily techniques such as meditation, conscious breathing, and mindful movement are bridges that connect us to reality. The more we use them, the more natural living in the present moment will become.

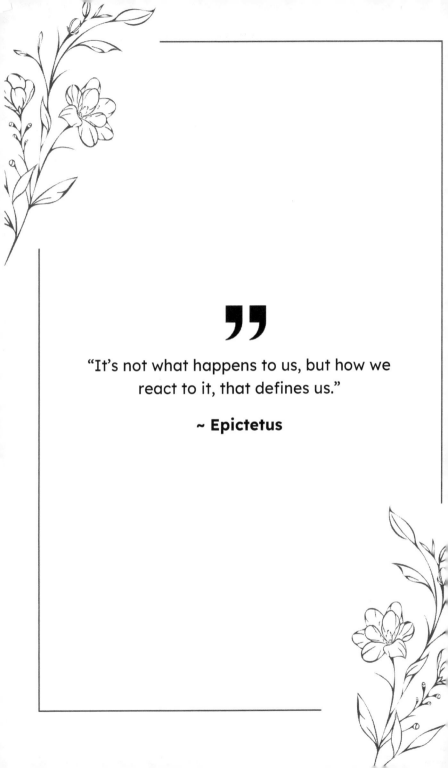

"It's not what happens to us, but how we react to it, that defines us."

~ Epictetus

Acceptance of Reality

Life rarely unfolds exactly as we plan it. Unexpected challenges, changes beyond our control, or a reality that falls short of our expectations can provoke frustration and anxiety. Yet, acceptance of reality is the key to inner peace. This does not mean passivity or resignation, but consciously embracing what is, rather than constantly fighting against what should be. Through acceptance, we stop wasting energy on unrealistic expectations and begin to live in harmony with what is happening right now.

The first step toward acceptance is mindfulness—being fully present in the current moment. Many of our worries stem from obsessively analyzing the past or fearing the future. Meanwhile, the only moment over which we have any control is the present. Focusing on what we see, hear, and feel in the moment opens us to reality as it is, without unnecessary filters or judgments. As Eckhart Tolle writes in *The Power of Now*: "You are not your thoughts, emotions, or past experiences. You are consciousness—here and now." Mindfulness practice teaches us that although we cannot control everything, we have complete control over how we react to what happens.

Acceptance of reality also requires flexibility—the ability to adapt to changes and challenges. Life is dynamic, and rigidly holding onto one plan often leads to frustration. Being flexible allows us to view difficulties from a different perspective, finding lessons and opportunities for growth. Imagine bamboo that bends in the wind but never breaks. It's this flexibility that helps us weather storms and emerge stronger. As the Stoic philosopher Epictetus observed: "It's not what happens to us, but how we react to it, that defines us."

Many of us live under the belief that happiness can only be achieved when we have complete control over our lives. However, the truth is that most things happening around us are beyond our control—from the weather to the decisions of others, and even unpredictable events. Trying to control everything leads us into a trap of frustration and anxiety. Acceptance involves letting go of this need. When we acknowledge that some things just happen, we can focus on what truly depends on us: our response.

In difficult times, it's helpful to remember that life is not only made up of bright moments but also shadows. These tougher moments often turn out to be our greatest teachers, showing us what within ourselves requires attention and change. Acceptance of reality is not surrender, but an act of courage. It's the ability to look at the world as it is and say to ourselves,

Unlock the Power of Now

"This is what I have in front of me. How can I make the most of this moment?" Only by letting go of the struggle with the inevitable do we open ourselves to peace, harmony, and a fuller experience of each moment of life.

Creating Harmony with Life

Life is a constant juggling act—work, family, obligations, and dreams. Balancing what we must do with what we want to do often seems impossible. However, harmony with life doesn't involve perfect balance, but rather the conscious creation of space that allows us to experience joy and fulfillment.

Everyday life can feel overwhelming, especially when the to-do list seems endless. The key is mastering time management, which not only helps us fulfill our responsibilities but also creates room for pleasure. One of the most effective techniques is the "time-blocking" method—planning the day in defined blocks, where alongside work and priority tasks, we make space for activities that bring joy. Whether it's a walk, a moment with a book, or a conversation with a loved one—these small moments of pleasure are like recharging our batteries. As Stephen R. Covey said in *The 7 Habits of Highly Effective People*: "What is most important should never be at the mercy of what is least important." Conscious planning allows us to find harmony, even on the busiest days.

Our worth doesn't come from what we possess, but from what we give to the world and how we impact the lives of others. Activities that build positive relationships, such as shared hobbies, volunteering, or simply being open to others, strengthen our sense of belonging and purpose. It's essential to remember that the quality of our relationships directly affects the quality of our lives. Research by psychologist Robert Waldinger, director of the long-term Harvard Study of Adult Development, has shown that people with strong, positive connections are healthier and more satisfied with life than those who lack them.

Building self-worth begins with us—it's about what we do for ourselves. Even small activities that give us a sense of achievement, such as regular exercise, learning new things, or pursuing creative ideas, help us build the inner belief that we are worthy of living life to its fullest.

Every day is an opportunity—a unique chance that will never come again. Living life to the fullest means finding joy in the small things, like a morning coffee, the laughter of a child, or the scent of rain. But it's also more than that: it's the courage to pursue our passions and desires. Many people put their dreams off until "someday"—when they have more time, money, or energy. The truth is, the perfect moment will never arrive.

Unlock the Power of Now

Take inspiration from J.K. Rowling, who wrote *Harry Potter* as a single mother, balancing the challenges of everyday life. Her determination to follow her passion despite adversity proves that even small steps toward our dreams can lead to great things.

Creating harmony with life isn't about perfection or eliminating problems. It's about the choices we make every day to feel that life is not just a series of duties, but also a space for laughter, love, and passion. Harmony is within reach if we choose it consciously. As Anthony de Mello said: "Happiness is not something that comes to you. It's something you create."

Four CHAPTER

MAINTAINING CHANGE OVER TIME

- Routine as the Foundation of Success
- Protecting Yourself from Falling Back into Old Habits
- Finding Joy in Every Day

Routine as the Foundation of Success

Change is not a sprint but a marathon, and routine is its map. Great achievements rarely stem from single bursts of inspiration; they are the result of consistency that gradually shapes our lives. If we want to live more consciously and fully experience the present moment, the key is to create habits that support our goals and values.

Every habit starts with a decision—the decision to change something in our lives and create space for what truly matters. At first, this might be as simple as turning off your phone for 10 minutes each day to focus on your breath or writing down one thing you're grateful for. The key is consistency—repeating these small actions until they become automatic.

James Clear, author of *Atomic Habits*, writes: "You do not rise to the level of your goals. You fall to the level of your systems." It is these small daily rituals that shape our reality. If you introduce even one habit that reminds you to live in the present moment, over time, you'll start noticing how much changes in your daily life.

You don't need to overhaul your entire life all at once. In fact, overly ambitious changes often lead to frustration and abandonment. Instead, focus on small, achievable goals. If you want to start meditating, begin with two minutes a day. If regular movement is important, try short walks rather than intense workouts.

Small steps are like bricks in a wall—initially insignificant, but over time, they build a solid structure. Mahatma Gandhi once said, "Be the change you want to see in the world." These words remind us that every change begins with a small, internal step.

Motivation is not something that magically appears every morning. Often, we must consciously seek it, especially on more difficult days. One of the best ways is to remind ourselves why we started. Ask yourself: What do I want to achieve? Why is this important to me? Hold onto your vision, even if the road seems bumpy.

In tougher moments, the reward method can be helpful. Break a large goal into smaller stages, and after completing each step, reward yourself with something you enjoy—a cup of your favorite coffee, watching a movie, or taking a short break to relax.

Unlock the Power of Now

It's also worth finding inspiration in the stories of people who have walked a similar path. Take Helen Keller, for example—a woman who, despite being completely blind and deaf, became one of the world's most influential writers and speakers. Her words, "Alone we can do so little, together we can do so much," remind us of the importance of support—from others and from ourselves.

Routine is not just repetition—it's a way to simplify life and focus energy on what truly matters. By creating small habits, taking incremental steps, and finding motivation in daily moments, you can build a foundation that will support you through any life situation. Remember, every great change starts with a small step. You can take that first step today.

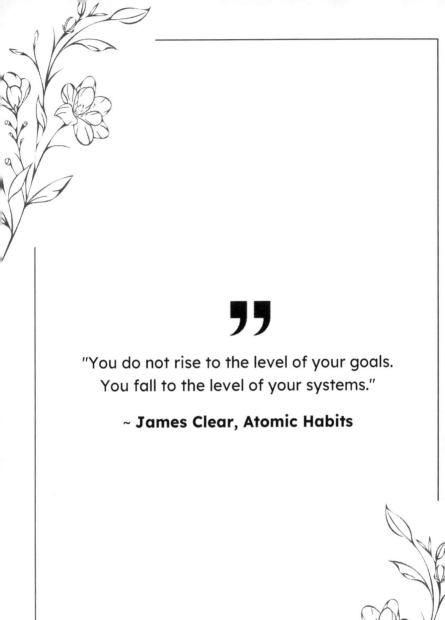

"You do not rise to the level of your goals.
You fall to the level of your systems."

~ **James Clear, Atomic Habits**

Protecting Yourself from Falling Back into Old Habits

Falling back into old habits is like pulling the emergency brake when you're already on the right track. At first, it may seem harmless—skipping one day of meditation, missing one workout, or spending an evening mindlessly scrolling through social media. But before you know it, small deviations begin to form a bigger pattern, and you find yourself back in the place you've been working so hard to escape. The key to protecting yourself from such regression is recognizing the warning signs. These may come in the form of moments when you start procrastinating, feeling overwhelmed by simple tasks, or experiencing an increasing desire to avoid challenges that once seemed easy to tackle. These signals are like warning lights on your dashboard—ignoring them can lead to much bigger issues.

One of the most effective tools in such moments is returning to your intentions. Remind yourself why you started. What inspired you to change? What promises did you make to yourself? A good practice could be writing a letter to your future self at the beginning of your journey, one that you can return to during moments of crisis. In this letter, you can express the emotions you're experiencing at the start of the journey—frustration, a desire to improve the quality of your life, or simply a longing for peace and balance. This letter becomes your personal compass, guiding you back to the right path when doubt arises.

Reminding yourself of the reasons for change is also a way to neutralize the pull of the past. The past often tries to "draw" us back into our old comfort zone, because the mind naturally seeks familiar solutions when faced with difficulties. To prevent this, you need rituals that help you maintain emotional and physical balance. These rituals don't need to be complicated—they can be small, yet regular actions. For example, starting your day with a moment of gratitude, writing down three things you're thankful for; a short meditation before bed to clear your mind; or a daily walk where you focus on your breath and the sounds of nature around you. These simple habits, when practiced regularly, hold great power.

Stephen Covey, author of The 7 Habits of Highly Effective People, said, "Our habits become our destiny." If you want to avoid falling back into old patterns, you must consciously take care of yourself on every level—physical, emotional, and mental. Regular physical activity not only improves your body's condition but also reduces stress and enhances your well-being. A healthy diet provides energy and influences your mood, while adequate sleep allows for regeneration and increases your ability to handle challenges.

Taking care of yourself also involves working with your emotions—rather than suppressing them, start noticing, accepting, and expressing them in ways that don't burden you. Try keeping a journal where you write down your thoughts and feelings. Writing helps you gain distance from your emotions and understand what triggers them. If you're struggling to name your emotions, think of them as waves in the ocean—they are part of life, coming and going, but you don't have to let them drown you.

Remember, every moment is a new opportunity to start again. Even if you temporarily fall back into old habits, don't treat it as a failure but as a lesson. Every step, even a backward one, is part of your process. The most important thing is to always remember where you're going and why this journey matters to you.

"

"Creating things that matter gives a sense of satisfaction that is hard to compare with anything else." **~ Steve Jobs**

Finding Joy in Every Day

Finding joy in every day is an art that can be mastered if we decide to live consciously. Conscious living is nothing more than fully immersing ourselves in the present moment, no matter what we're doing. Often, in the pursuit of the future or in reflecting on the past, we forget how important the here and now is. As Eckhart Tolle, author of *The Power of Now*, says: "A person who lives fully in the present moment is not burdened by the past or the future." It is in this moment that true joy resides—by appreciating the small, everyday moments that often slip by unnoticed in the rush of life.

Passion is one of the keys to living consciously. What you love doing gives you not only satisfaction but also a sense of purpose. Whether it's painting, playing an instrument, cooking, or even running, dedicating time to your passions allows you to dive deeper into the present. These are the moments when you forget everything around you and fully immerse yourself in what you're doing. Practicing your passion creates what can be called a "positive loop," where the joy of doing what you love motivates you to keep going. Steve Jobs, the creator of Apple, emphasized this when talking about his passion for technology, saying, "Creating things that matter gives a sense of satisfaction that is hard to compare with anything else."

Taking pleasure in simple things is another element that makes life joyful. Many people wait for big, breakthrough moments, but the truth is that real magic lies in the small things—in the taste of your favorite coffee, in laughter with a loved one, in a walk through the park, in the warm sun on your face. Pause for a moment to appreciate what you have now, rather than constantly striving for something you don't yet have. Being present in each moment means freeing yourself from the constant worry about what might happen and allowing yourself to fully experience what's happening right now.

An important aspect of finding joy in life is also sharing that joy with others. By sharing positive energy, we not only influence others but also ourselves. Every act of kindness, every moment when we can share a good word or deed, returns to us as a source of satisfaction. Spreading positive energy in our relationships with others is a way to build deeper, more authentic connections. It could be a smile to a stranger, helping someone in need, or just having a conversation that lifts your spirits. By sharing our joy, we learn to see it in others, which ultimately deepens our own satisfaction with life.

Unlock the Power of Now

So, how can you live more fully? Do what you love. Stop and appreciate the little things that bring you joy. Share that joy with others, because there is nothing more fulfilling than making an impact on someone who in turn shares their energy with you. And when you do this, you become part of a greater circle—not only taking care of yourself but also influencing the world around you.

CONCLUSION

Living in the present moment is the most powerful tool we have for healing. Instead of carrying the weight of the past, which is already gone, and the uncertainty of the future, which has not yet arrived, we have the opportunity to focus on what truly matters—right here, right now. In this present moment lies our true power. How we live in the present has a profound impact on our well-being, mental and emotional health. Day by day, we can choose to live more fully, joyfully, and in harmony with ourselves. Right now, in this very moment, the process of change begins, allowing us to heal our bodies, minds, and hearts.

In this book, I have presented tools and techniques to help you break free from the past and the uncertainty of the future. We began by understanding the immense role our perception of time plays, how the past can paralyze us and the future can frighten us. We then discovered how practicing presence can be the key to a life full of joy and peace. We learned how changing our thinking and practicing mindfulness daily can help overcome internal blocks, as well as how simple techniques like meditation, breathing, and affirmations can be the foundation of our journey toward inner harmony. Finally, we learned how to create lasting changes in our lives by eliminating old habits and replacing them with ones that support our new, present-centered reality.

Living in the present is not something that can be achieved overnight. It is a process that requires time, practice, and patience. But it is also a path that leads to true freedom—the freedom from fears, anxiety, and the burdens of the past. When you finish reading this book, remember that change has already begun within you. Every small step, every moment of mindfulness, every conscious decision brings you closer to a life full of joy, passion, and fulfillment.

Thank you for taking the time to read this book. I hope you find inspiration and tools here to create the life you truly deserve. I wish you the best of luck on your journey of transformation ahead. Remember, the most important moment is the one that is now. Live fully, be aware of every moment, and open yourself to the infinite possibilities of the present moment.

If this book has helped you at any point on your journey, I would be grateful if you would share your feedback on Amazon. Your review will help others find their way to a life in the present and transform their lives for the better.

With best wishes,

Rafael Lumnis

Resources:

1. Tolle, E. (2010). The power of now: A Guide to Spiritual Enlightenment. New World Library.

2. Mandela, N. (2008). Long walk to freedom: The Autobiography of Nelson Mandela. Hachette UK.

3. Brown, B. (2022). The gifts of imperfection: Let Go of Who You Think You're Supposed to Be and Embrace Who You Are. Simon and Schuster.

4. Kabat-Zinn, J. (2016). Wherever you go, there you are: Mindfulness meditation for everyday life. Hachette UK.

5. Covey, S. R. (1997). The Seven Habits of Highly Effective People: Restoring the Character Ethic. Macmillan Reference USA.

6. Clear, J. (2018). Atomic habits: An Easy & Proven Way to Build Good Habits & Break Bad Ones. Penguin.